This book belongs to:

..............................................................

Dirección editorial: Ana Delgado
Supervisión de los textos: Carole Patton
Asesoramiento y apoyo académico: Carlota Arroyo,
Niko Domínguez
Maquetación y diseño: Estelle Talavera
Ilustraciones: Francisca Valiente (texto),
Cristina de Cos-Estrada (vocabulario)


c/ Campezo, 13 - 28022 Madrid
Tel. 91 300 91 00 - Fax: 91 300 91 18
www.susaeta.com

D.L.: M-19909-MMXIV

EASY READING

# Pirates

susaeta

one

# PIRATES

The Golden Age of Piracy began in the 16th century. PIRATES sailed across the seas and oceans of the world, terrorizing everybody.

They didn't stop attacking ships until the 19th century. They STOLE everything they could and gathered enormous treasures.

PIRATES controlled Madagascar, Bahamas, Jamaica and Tortuga Island. They became so dominant in the area that... they seemed to RULE the islands!

In the Caribbean Sea, SPANISH ships CARRIED gold and treasures from America back home. PIRATES couldn't resist temptation.

Let's meet the PIRATES.

What did they look like? They didn't use to be very clean... And they wore hats to protect themselves from the sun.

They always CARRIED their *pistols* with them... and sometimes, even a hidden knife too.

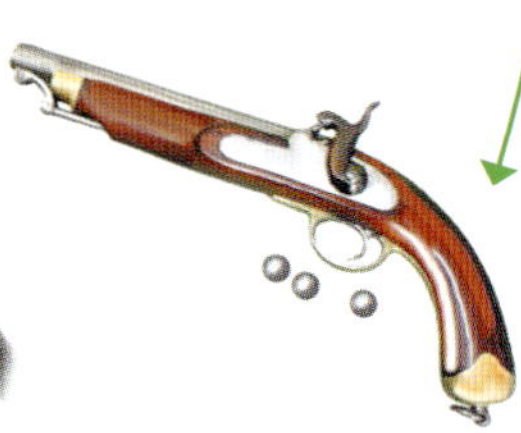

They often LACKED a hand or a leg, as a result of the battles. They could even lose an eye!

If they lost an eye, they wore a patch.

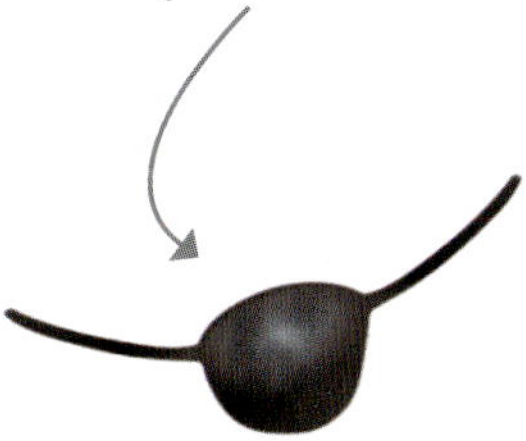

If they lost a leg, they used a WOODEN LEG.

If they lost a hand, they would use a HOOK.

They used to adopt parrots and monkeys.

And they CARRIED cats on the ships to keep them free of rats.

Rats often made holes in the ships' hulls! That was very dangerous, the ships could FLOOD and sink.

TWO

# ON THE SHIP

The most important person on the ship was the Captain. He had to be fierce and he also had to be a great leader, for he needed all members of the CREW to follow his orders.

Ship travels were very hard: the burning sun during the day and the freezing cold during the night, the storms, the dirt, the DISEASES, the LACK of water and food.
And **shipwrecks**...

PIRATES preferred smaller ships. They were faster and easier to sail.

Between 30 and 50 PIRATES would travel on each pirate ship.
They needed to choose cleverly what to CARRY with them on the ship. They were going to travel for many many days!

But above all, they would need WATER.

They needed fresh water to survive, but PIRATES loved rum! They even used it to disinfect WOUNDS...

In every pirate ship there was a boatswain. He was the captain's right hand. He distributed food, drink and **WEAPONS**, and he was also the one who administered punishments if necessary.

The **SURGEON** was also essential. He wasn't always a real doctor, but it was better than nothing...

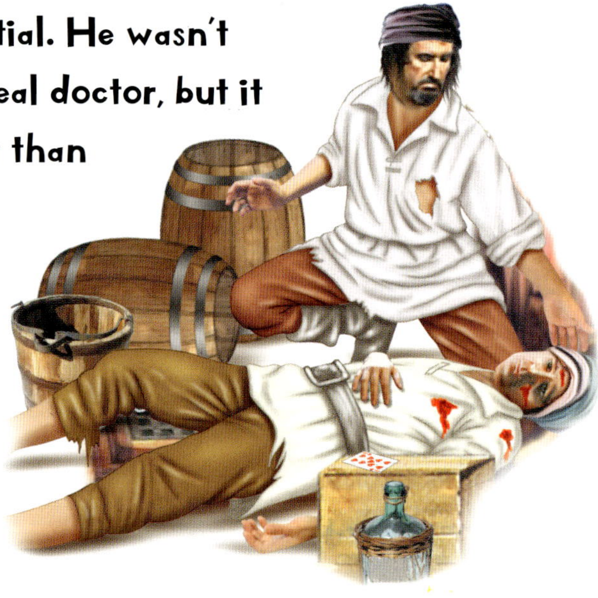

The gunner had to use the cannons very well. They fired the enemy's ship to slow down its speed.

There was a strict code of **BEHAVIOUR** on the ship. Scammers were severely punished.

Keeping water fresh could sometimes be tricky and became an important problem: over time, it could get bad and cause infections. Luckily the American natives told them how to solve the problem using corn flour.

Their most common food was a type of hard cookie that was often filled with bugs... How disgusting!

And what did PIRATES eat?
They had to travel for so many days that they could only CARRY potatoes, cereal, dried beans, smoked meat and cookies on the ship.

They also had chickens, so they could eat eggs every day.

When they arrived at a port, they would buy some fruit and vegetables, but these didn't **last** very long, because they were difficult to keep fresh and in good conditions.

And, certainly, they would fish whenever they could.

## Three

# REWARDS AND PUNISHMENTS

When a PIRATE managed to SPOT a ship in the distance, or if he was the first to step on an enemy ship, a reward was given to him.

But the best rewards were new navigation maps. A detailed map could bring new, interesting routes.

All PIRATES had to help each other in the FIGHT. Not following that RULE would bring terrible punishments, inflicted by the rest of the CREW.

When SPANISH, BRITISH or FRENCH ships captured a PIRATE, they would cut his head off and show it off, as a warning for the rest...

Money **BETTING** was also forbidden on board.

But the worst punishment was the so-called 'marooning': to be abandoned on a small desert island, distant from any navigation route, with a bottle of rum, a can of water, a gun and one BULLET. In most cases, the marooned PIRATE would get drunk and take his own life.

FOUR

# PIRATE ISLAND

The greatest concentration of PIRATES was on Tortuga Island. There they had their own laws: there were no prejudices for nationality or religion; there was no private property and individual freedom was respected; there were no obligations or punishments. Women weren't allowed there.

Any ship that approached the island, instantly became property of all the PIRATES.

Turtle soup was one of the PIRATES' favourite foods.

In the 17th century there was a port in Jamaica that was a real pirate's nest: Port Royal.
It was full of TAVERNS.

FIGHTS were constant there.
PIRATES were terribly RUDE and had no respect for women.

TAVERN

Five

# THE BATTLE

**PIRATES** were more feared than storms... And even more if there was a red flag with a **SKULL** on the ship. It meant: "No life will be **SPARED**."

They also made explosives they would throw as grenades. While the enemy tried to hide, the PIRATES would jump on the enemy's ship.

Many deaths were caused in the battle.

Six

# STORMS

If a PIRATE was afraid of something, that would be the terrible storms that were sometimes formed in the Caribbean Sea. Their ships were small and tropical storms TORE them easily.

The tropical hurricane wind can reach 300 kilometres per hour! **WAVES** could get as big as a 10-storey building!

The sails had to be picked up quickly as the storm began.

Everyone must be on DECK during the storm, and hold onto something to avoid falling into the sea.

If the storm caught them near the SHORE, it SHATTERED them against the rocks.

Seven

# THE END OF THE GOLDEN AGE OF PIRACY

**During August, September and October, PIRATES preferred to attack COASTAL cities better than ships, because there were many tropical storms during those months in the Caribbean.**

**In the early 16th century, a single storm sent 20 ships to the sea bed.**

In 1716, there were about 2,000 PIRATES. From that moment, they were CHASED TIRELESSLY, especially by the BRITISH. In 1725 there were only 200 PIRATES left.

# VOCABULARY

## PIRATE VOCABULARY:

**Ahoy!** 'Hello!'

**Arr!** An exclamation.

**Aye!** 'Yes!'

**Jolly Roger** The famous flag with skull and bones.

**Sail ho!** Expression used to say a ship is in view.

**Seadog** An old sailor.

**Shiver me timbers!** Expression used to show surprise.

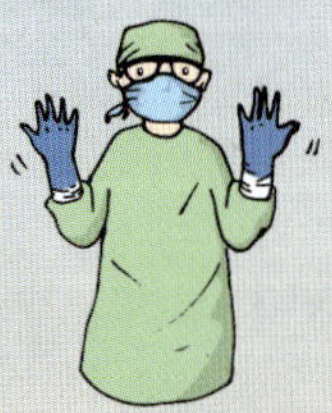

SURGEON

STEAL (p. STOLE)

shipwreck

WAVE

reward

Deck

FIGHT

SHORE

sails

hull

sink

corn flour

- **ASSAULT** A violent physical attack.
- **BEHAVIOUR** To act in a suitable way, to conduct oneself (well).
- **BETTING** An agreement between two parties that a sum of money or other stake will be paid by the loser to the party.
- **boatswain** A petty officer on a merchant ship who is responsible for the maintenance of the ship and its equipment.
- **can** A usually cylindrical metal container.
- **CARRY** To move or take from one place to another; transport.
- **CHASE** To run after someone or something.
- **COASTAL** Next to the sea; the seashore.
- **CREW** All of a ship's personnel.
- **DISEASE** A disorder of an organ or another part of a body resulting from the effect of infection or toxicity; illness; sickness.
- **FLOOD** To become inundated, covered with water.
- **gather** To collect from different places.
- **gunner** One who hunts or kills with a gun.

- **LACK** Deficiency or absence.
- **last** To remain in good condition.
- **pick up** To collect, to lift something up.
- **punish** To inflict a punishment, a penalty, for an offense or fault.
- **RUDE** Impolite, disrespectful, bad-mannered.
- **RULE** An authoritative, prescribed direction for conduct. A legal doctrine or principle.
- **scammer** A person who commits fraud.
- **SHATTER** To destroy or ruin something.
- **TIRELESSLY** Not stopping or taking a rest of something.
- **solve** To find the explanation for or solution to a mystery or a problem.
- **SPARE** To avoid injuring or killing someone.
- **SPOT** To detect or discern, especially visually.
- **TEAR** (*p.* TORE) To pull apart or into pieces by force; rend.
- **used to** In the habit of doing something frequently in the past but not any more in the present.
- **wound** Any break in the skin or an organ or part as the result of violence or a surgical incision.

# ARE THESE SENTENCES CORRECT?

1 • Pirates used to be very clean and kind with women.

☐ YES ☐ NO

2 • All pirates had to help each other in the fight. Not following that rule would bring terrible punishments.

☐ YES ☐ NO

3 • Money betting was the best thing to do on board. And it was allowed.

☐ YES ☐ NO

4 • A red flag with a skull on the ship meant: "We don't have any diseases."

☐ YES ☐ NO

# COMPLETE THESE SENTENCES WITH THE CORRECT WORD.

1 • Pirates needed fresh water to survive, but they also loved rum! They even used it to disinfect ______________.

2 • Pirate ships were small and tropical storms ______________ them easily.

3 • Rats often made holes in the ______________!

4 • In the early 16th century a single ______________ sent 20 ships to the sea bed.

5 • The ______________ had to be picked up quickly as the storm began.

WAVE hull

WOUNDS sails TORE